ANIMAL PATTERNS

Compiled by Jean Warren

Illustrated by Gary Mohrmann

Warren Publishing House, Inc.
Everett, Washington

Editorial Staff: Gayle Bittinger, Susan M. Sexton, Jean Warren

Production Staff: Eileen Carbary, Kathy Jones

Computer Graphics: André Gene Samson, Eric Stovall

ISBN: 0-911019-31-6

Printed in the United States of America
Published by: Warren Publishing House, Inc.
P.O. Box 2250
Everett, Washington 98203

CONTENTS

Suggestions for Using Animal Patterns

Mix and match the patterns in this book to create a variety of teaching props, learning games, bulletin boards and more. Following are some suggestions of ways to use the patterns. Adapt these ideas or make up your own—the only limit is your imagination.

Language

Flannelboard Story Characters—Use the patterns as guides to cut animal shapes out of felt or construction paper backed with felt strips.

Stick Puppets—Color and cut out photocopies of the smallest animal shapes and glue them to Popsicle sticks or tongue depressors.

Stand-up Story Characters—Use the patterns as guides to cut animal shapes out of posterboard. Make stands for the shapes out of posterboard or playdough.

Magnetic Story Characters—Use the patterns as guides to cut animal shapes out of construction paper or posterboard and attach magnets to the backs of them.

Picture Books—Photocopy several animal shapes of the same size, arrange them in the desired order and staple them together to make books. Add construction paper covers, if desired.

Draw-A-Story—Cut out several photocopied shapes, cover them with clear self-stick paper and put them in a bag or a box. Let the children take turns pulling out a shape for you to incorporate into a story.

Music and Movement

Finger Puppets—Color and cut out photocopies of the smallest animal shapes and attach them to construction paper or pipe cleaner "rings." Use the finger puppets while reciting animal poems or singing animal songs.

"Act Like Me" Game—Photocopy and cut out several animal shapes and cover them with clear self-stick paper. Put them in a bag or a box. Let the children take turns drawing an animal shape out of the bag and acting like that animal while the other children try to guess what it is.

Animal Songs—Use the patterns as guides to cut animal shapes of construction paper or felt. Use the shapes as props while singing songs about animals.

Learning Games

Matching—Use the patterns as guides to cut various sizes and kinds of animal shapes out of construction paper or felt. Let the children match the shapes by size, color or animal.

Counting—Use the patterns as guides to cut various sizes and kinds of animal shapes out of construction paper or felt. Ask the children to count the large shapes, the red shapes or all of the horse shapes.

Sizing—Use the patterns as guides to cut four sizes of one animal's shape out of construction paper or felt. Have the children arrange the shapes by size.

Sorting—Use the patterns as guides to cut various sizes and kinds of animal shapes out of construction paper or felt. Let the children sort the shapes by animal, size, color, feature (tail, nose, legs, etc.) or habitat.

Card Games—Photocopy and cut out the game cards. Cover them with clear self-stick paper. Help the children use the cards to play such games as Go Fish, Concentration, Lotto and Bingo.

Art

Stencils—Use the patterns as guides to cut animal shapes out of large pieces of posterboard or tag board to make stencils.

Necklaces—Use the patterns as guides to cut animal shapes out of construction paper. Let the children each decorate one or more shapes. String each child's shapes on a piece of yarn.

Stamps—Use the patterns as guides to cut animal shapes out of sponges. Glue the sponge shapes to blocks of wood to make stamps.

Classroom Aids

Room Decorations—Use the patterns as guides to cut out animal shapes for decorating bulletin boards or creating a frieze.

Calendar Markers—Use one of the smaller patterns as a guide to cut animal shapes, one for each day of the month, out of construction paper. Number the shapes and arrange them in a calendar format on a bulletin board.

Name Tags—Use the patterns as guides to cut animal shapes out of construction paper. Write a child's name on each shape and string it on a piece of yarn.

Alligator 7

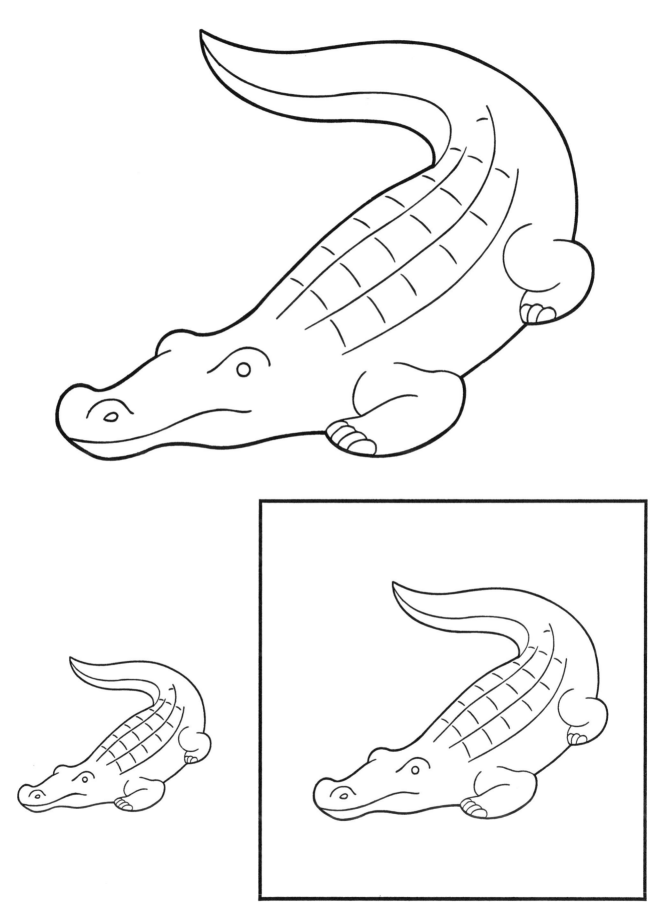

Alligator 9

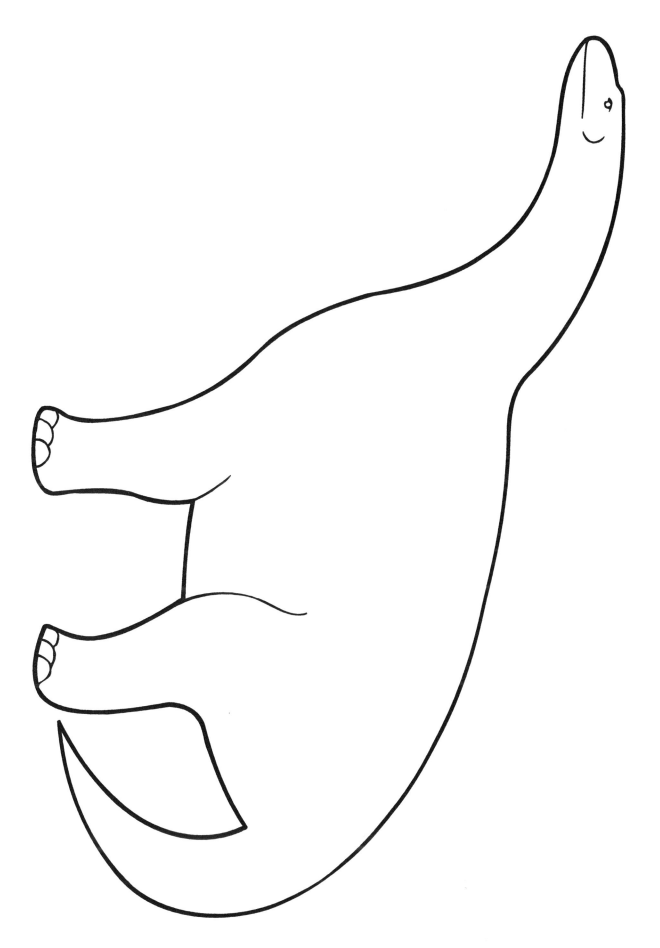

Apatosaurus 11

Apatosaurus 13

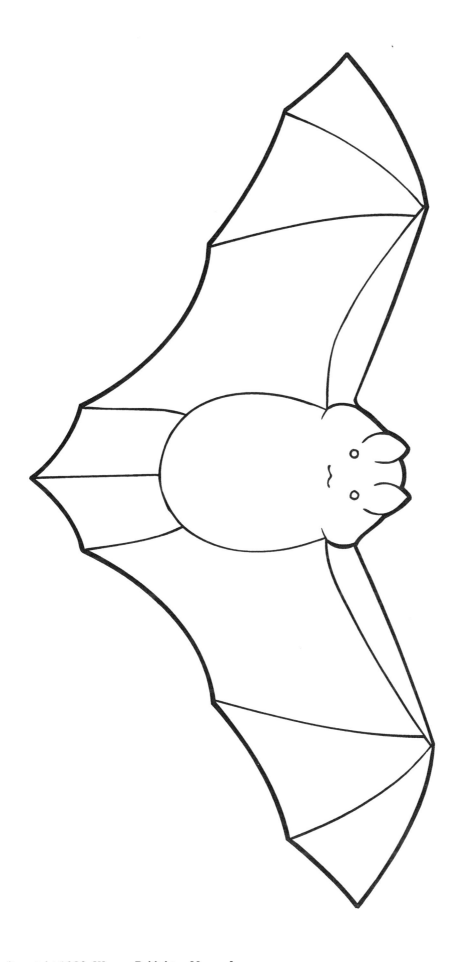

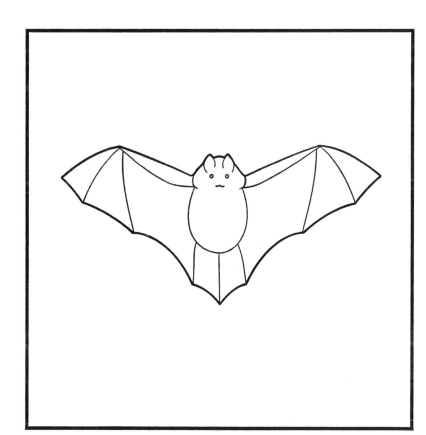

Bat 17

Bear 19

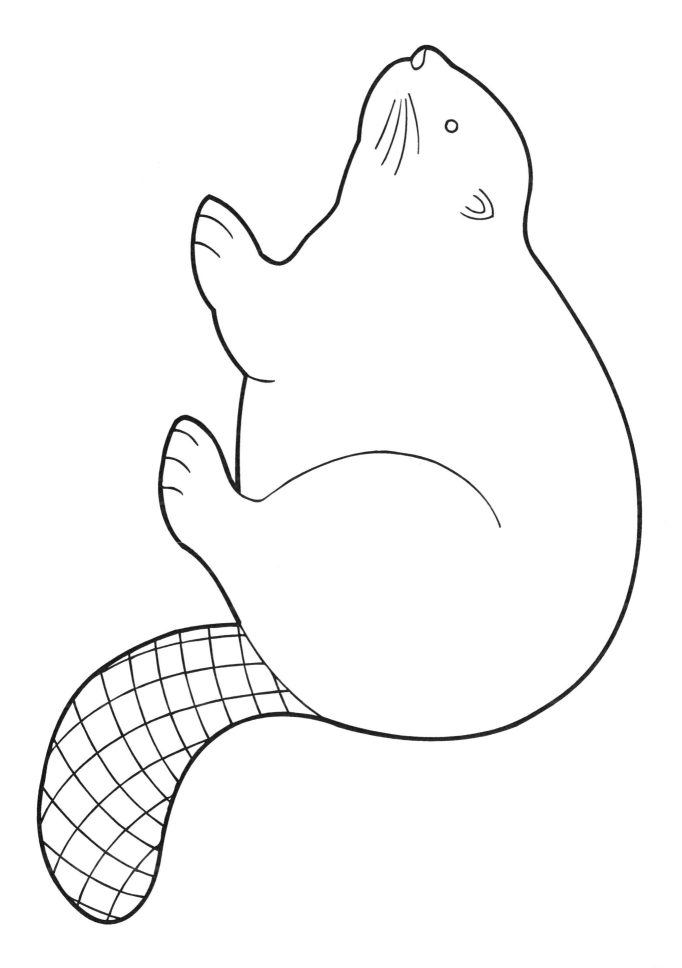

Beaver   23

Beaver 25

Bee 27

Bird 31

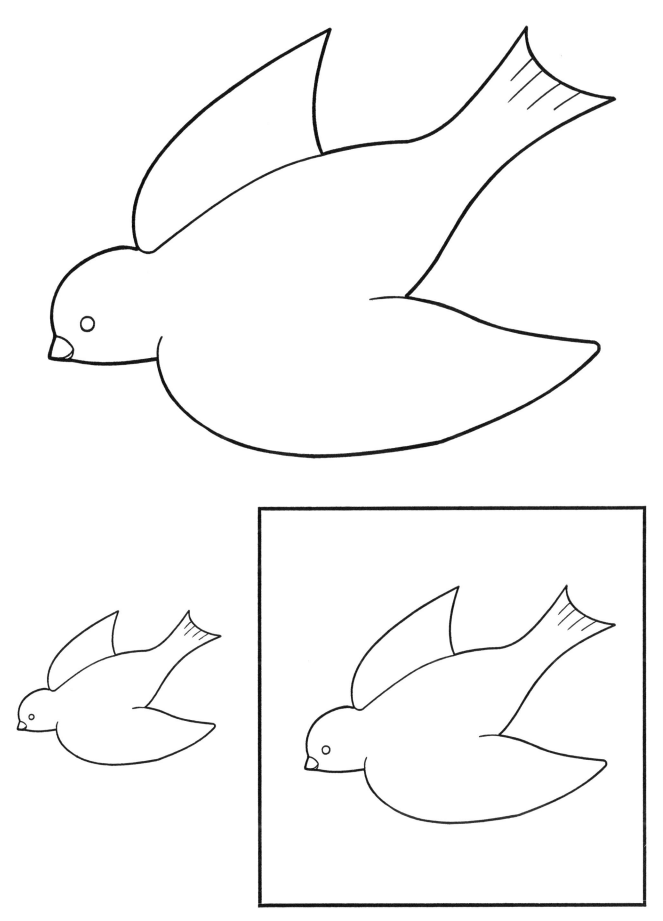

Bird 33

Buffalo 35

Buffalo 37

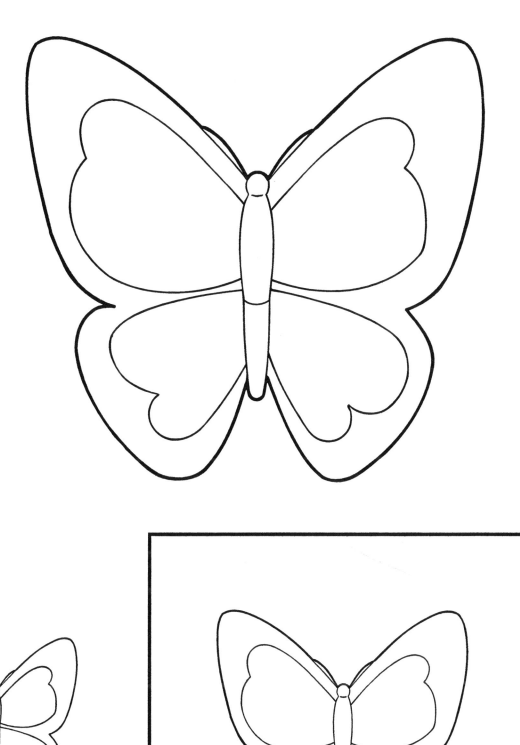

Butterfly 41

Camel 43

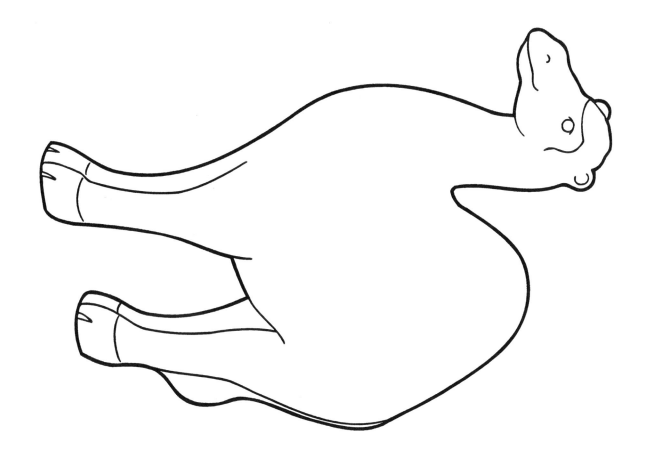

Cat 47

Cat 49

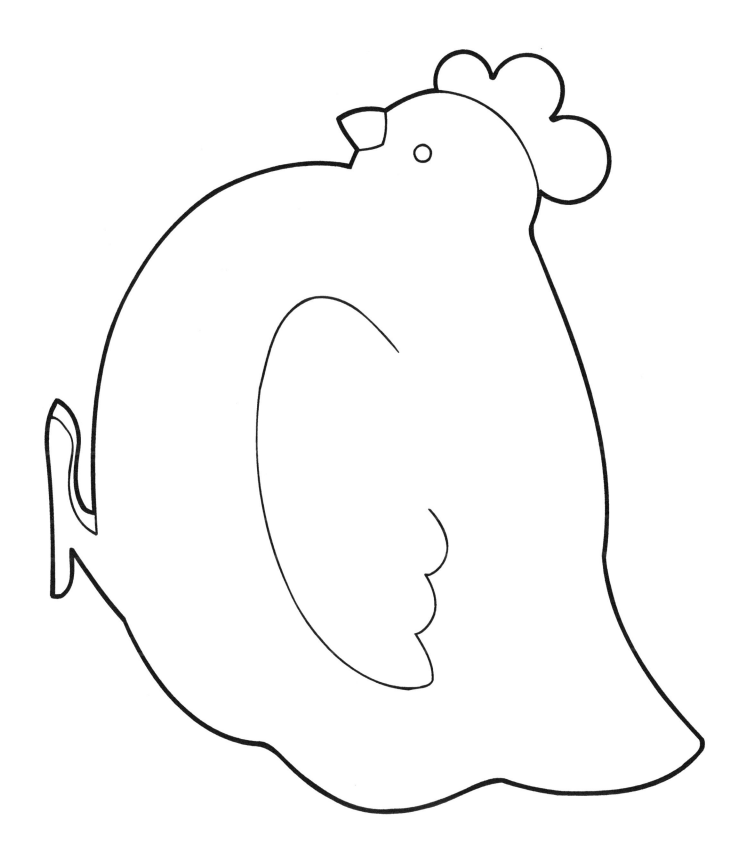

Chicken 51

Chicken 53

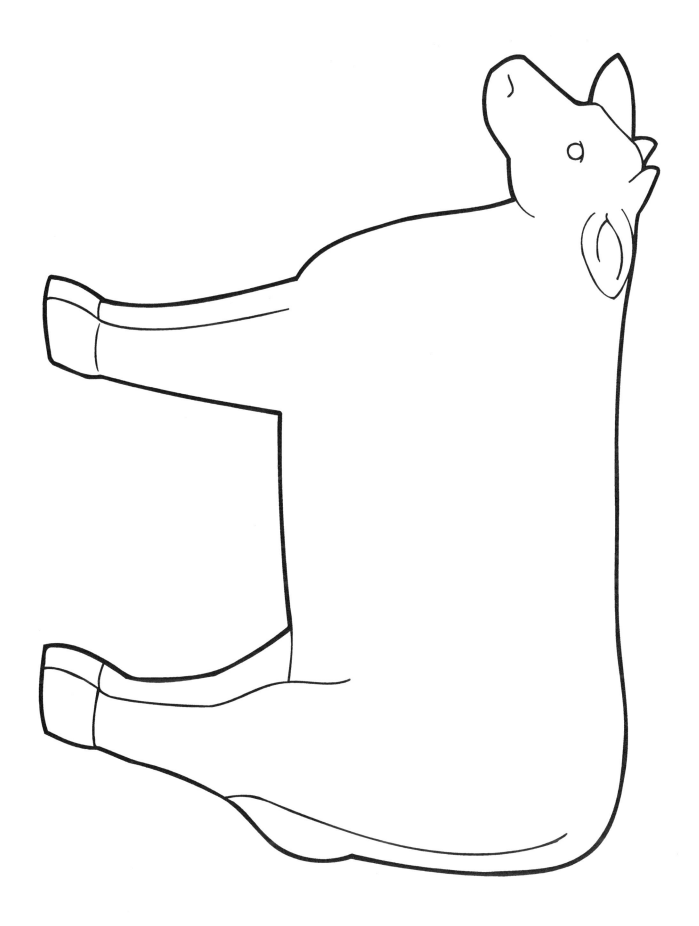

Cow 55

Cow 57

Deer 61

Dog 63

Dog 65

Donkey 67

Donkey 69

Duck 71

Duck 73

Elephant 75

Elephant 77

Fish 79

Fish 81

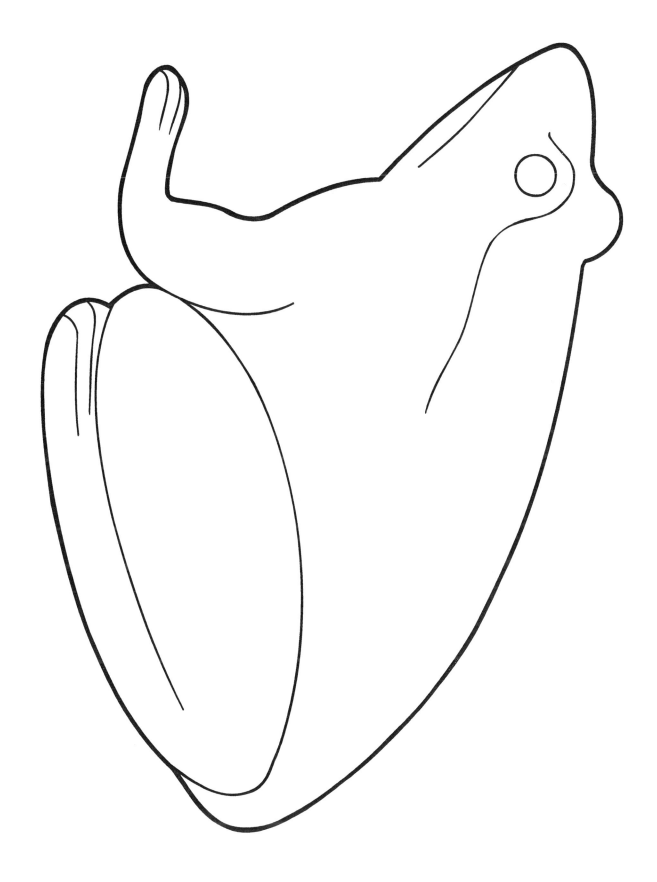

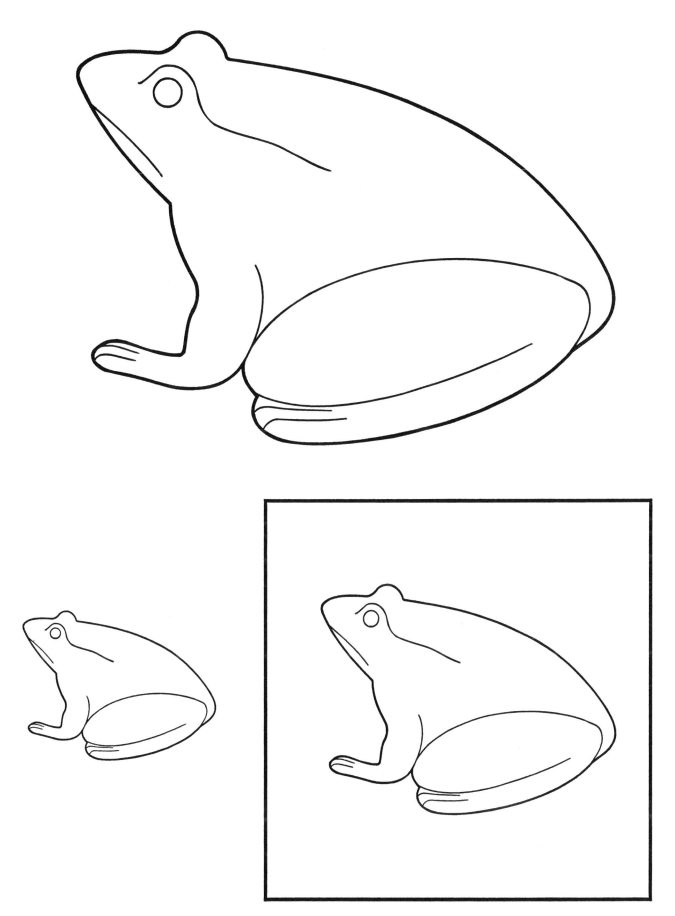

Frog 89

Giraffe 91

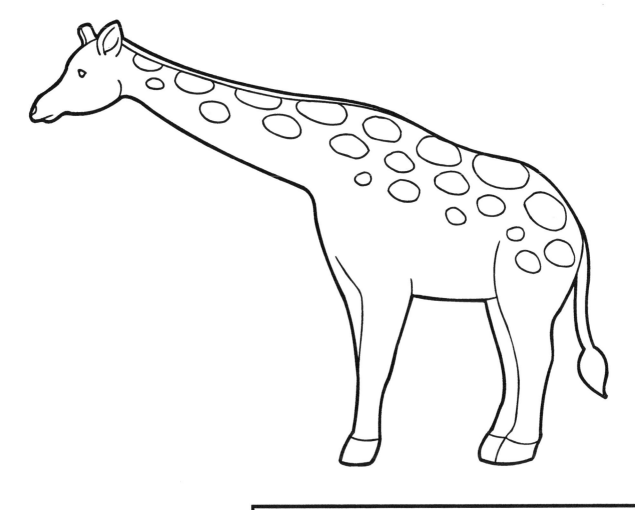

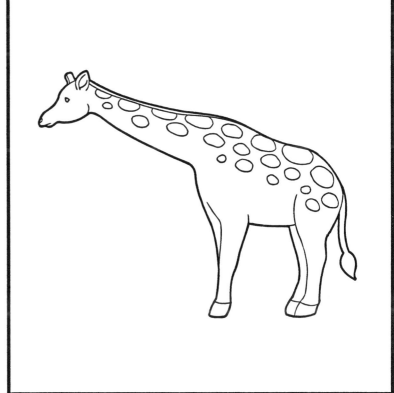

Giraffe 93

Goose 95

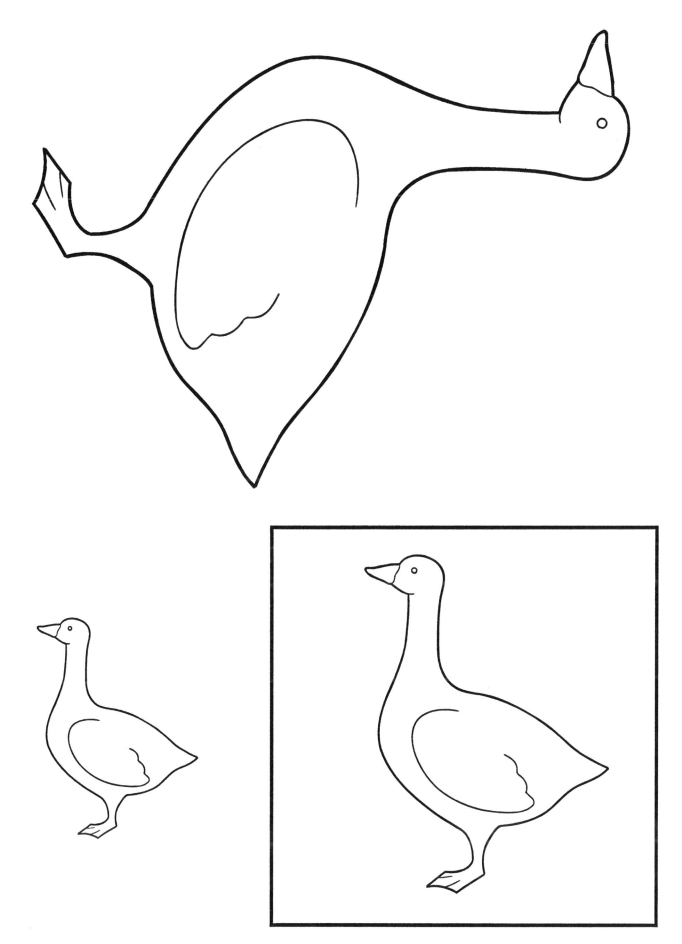

Goose 97

Gorilla 99

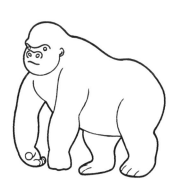

Hippopotamus 103

Hippopotamus   105

Horse 107

Horse 109

Kangaroo 111

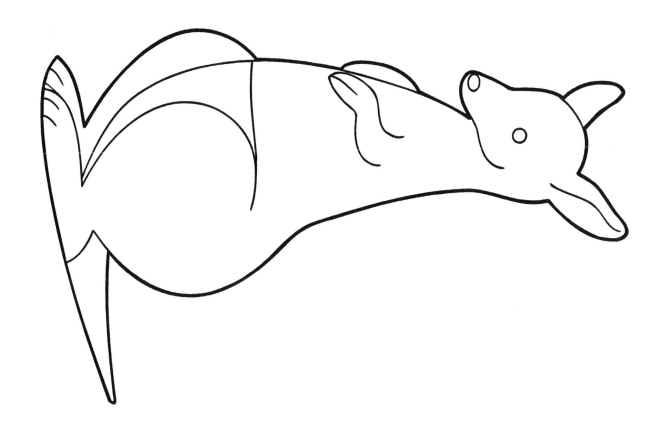

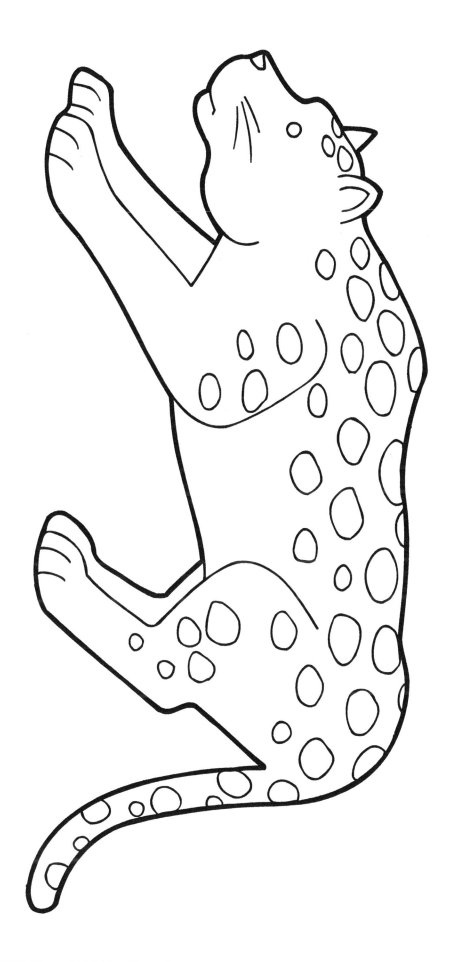

Leopard 115

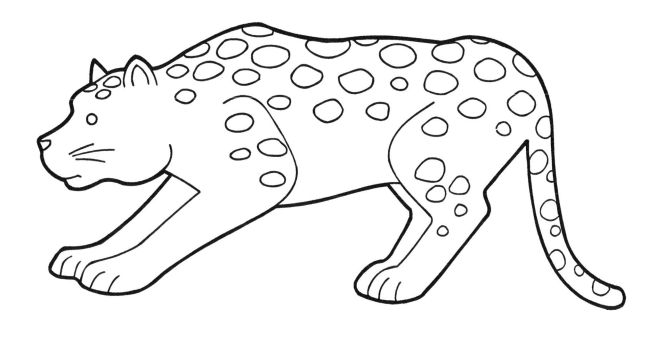

Lion   119

Lion 121

Monkey 123

Monkey 125

Mouse 127

Octopus 131

Octopus 133

Ostrich   135

Ostrich 137

Owl 139

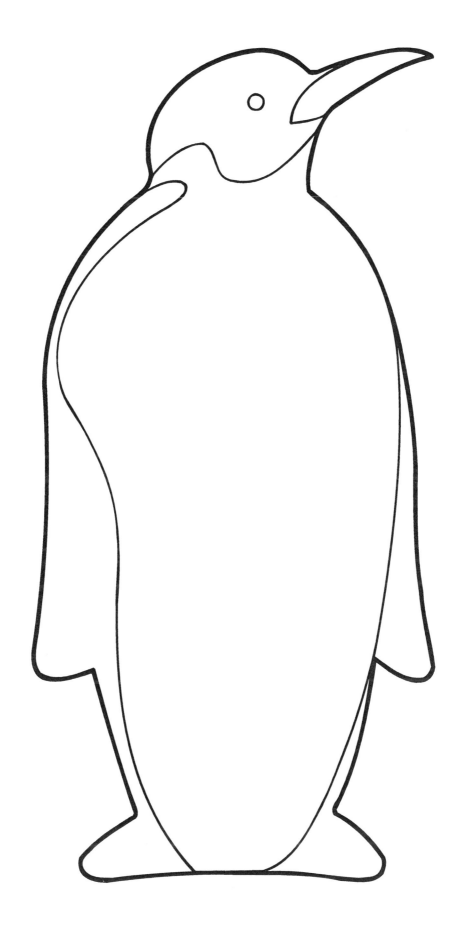

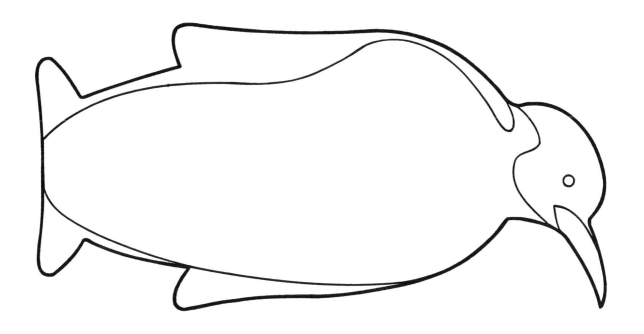

Penguin 145

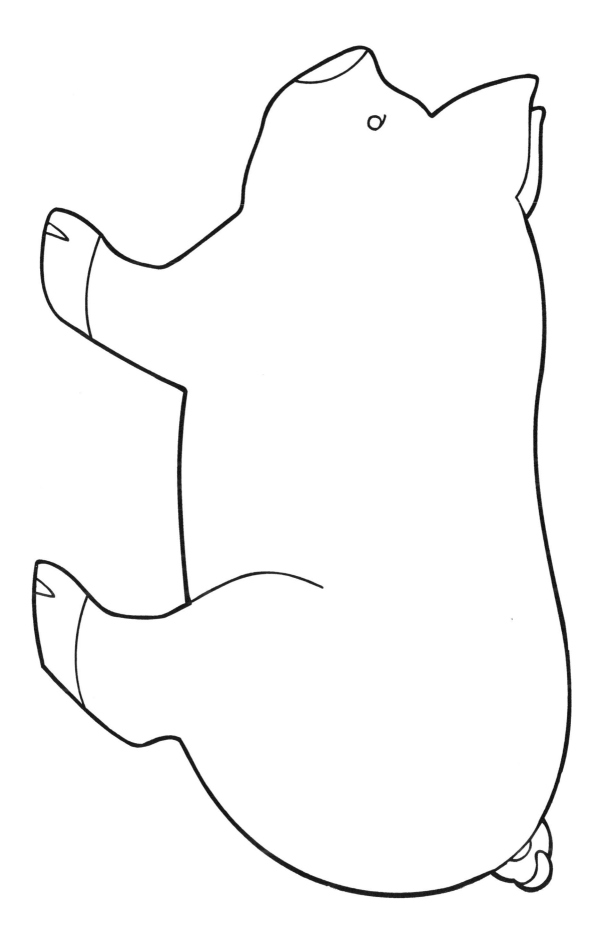

Pig 147

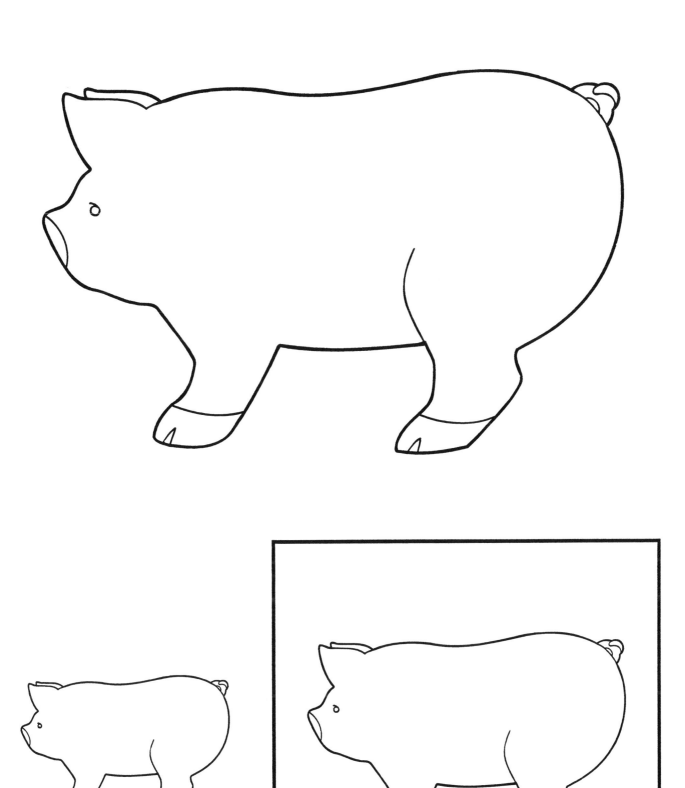

Pig 149

Rabbit 151

Rabbit 153

Raccoon 155

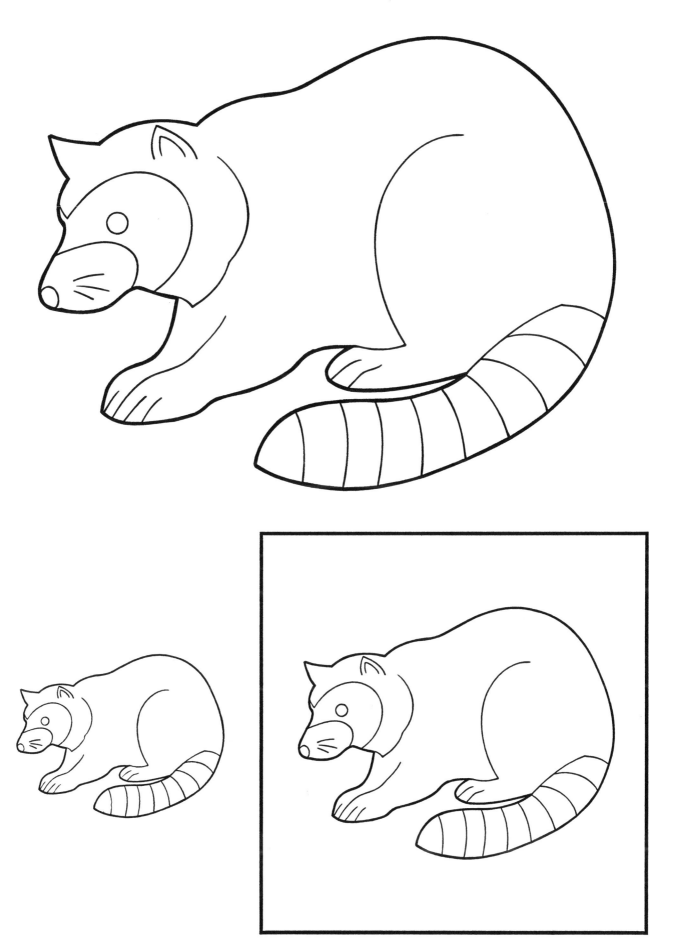

Raccoon 157

Rhinoceros   159

Rhinoceros 161

Rooster   163

Rooster 165

Sea Gull   167

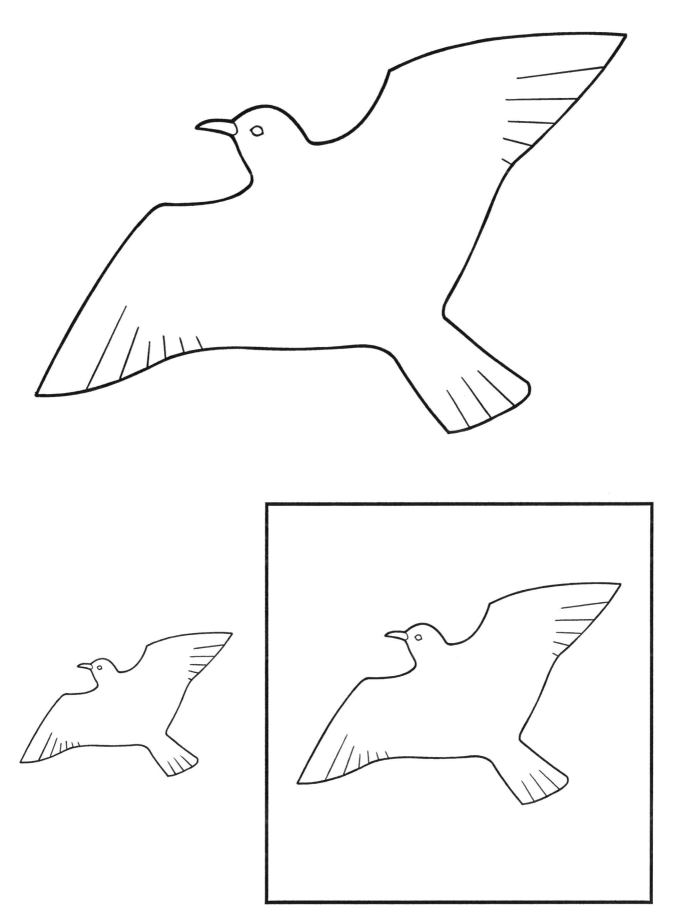

Sea Gull 169

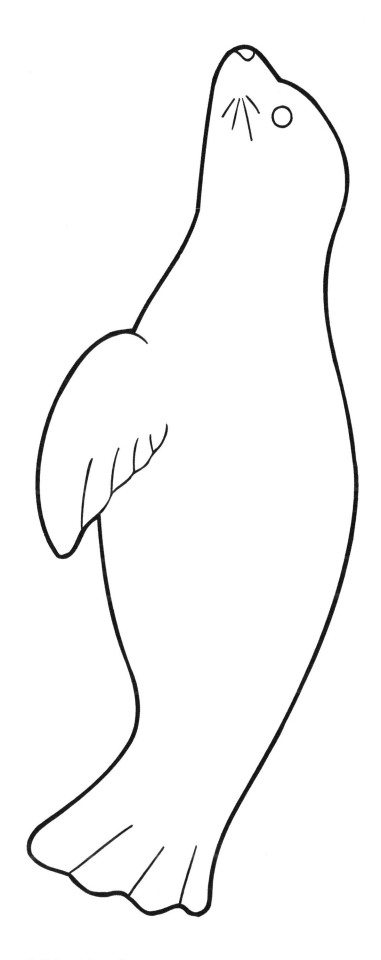

Seal 171

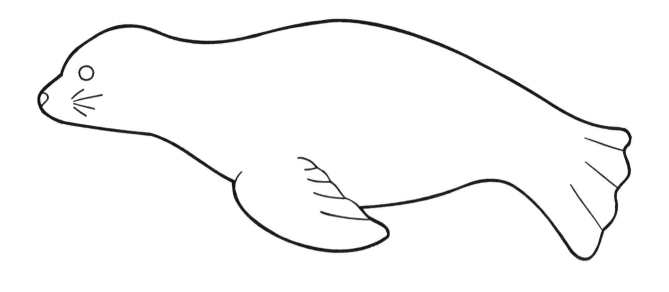

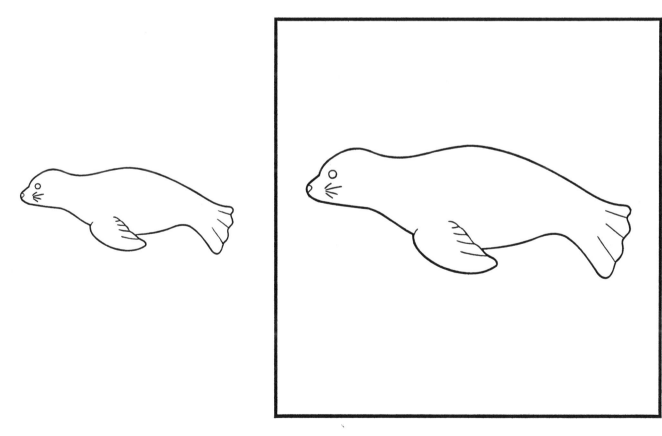

Seal 173

Shark 175

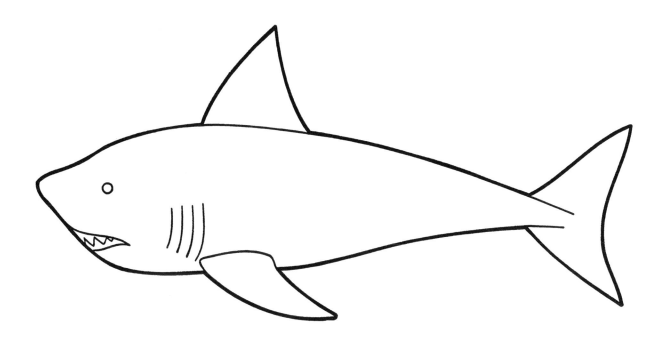

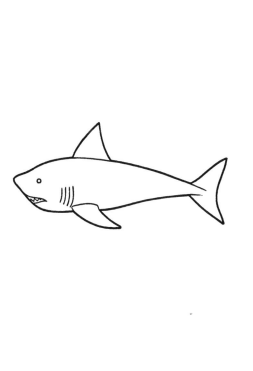

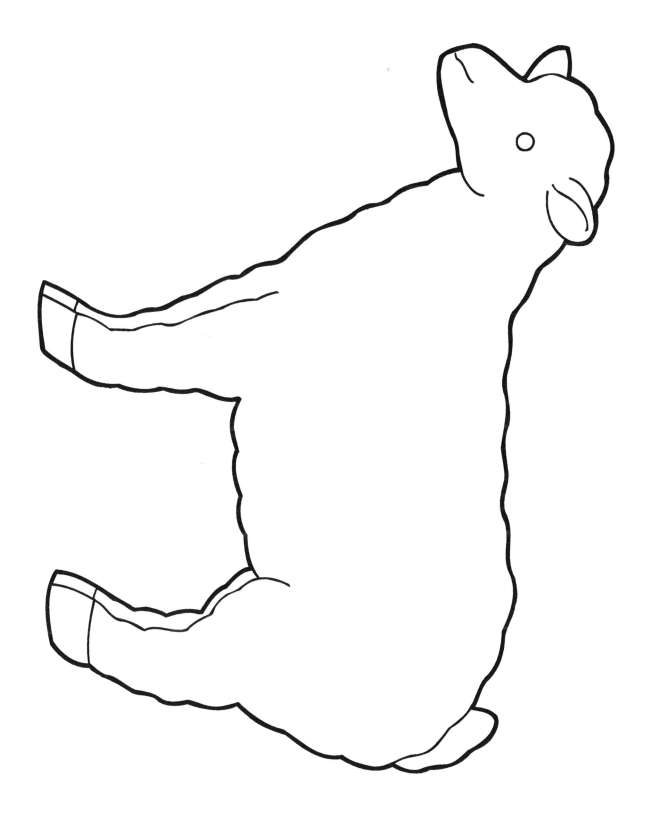

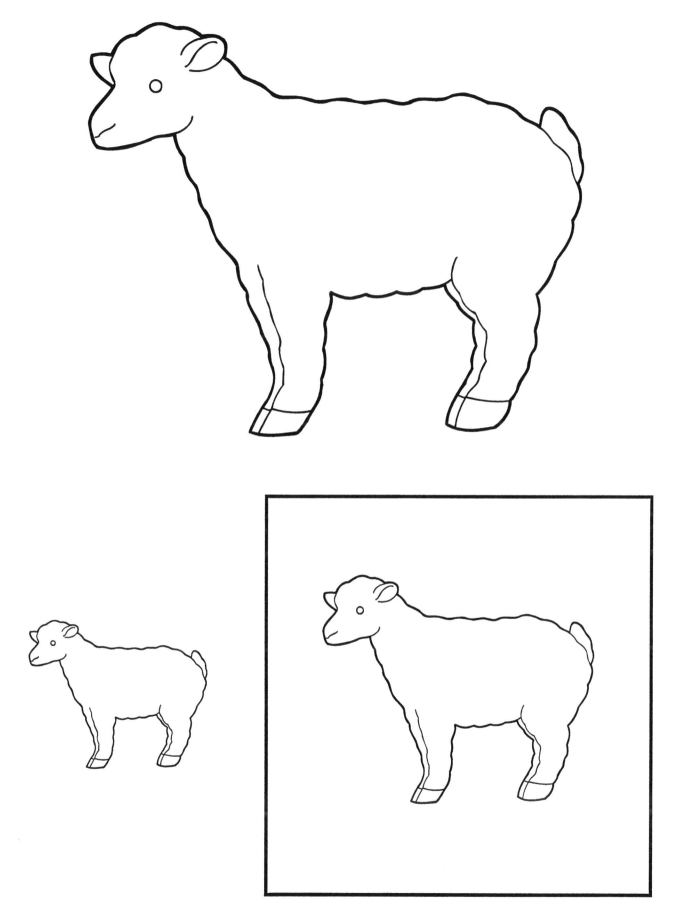

Sheep 181

Skunk 183

Skunk 185

Snail   187

Snail 189

Snake 191

Snake 193

Squirrel 195

Stegosaurus 199

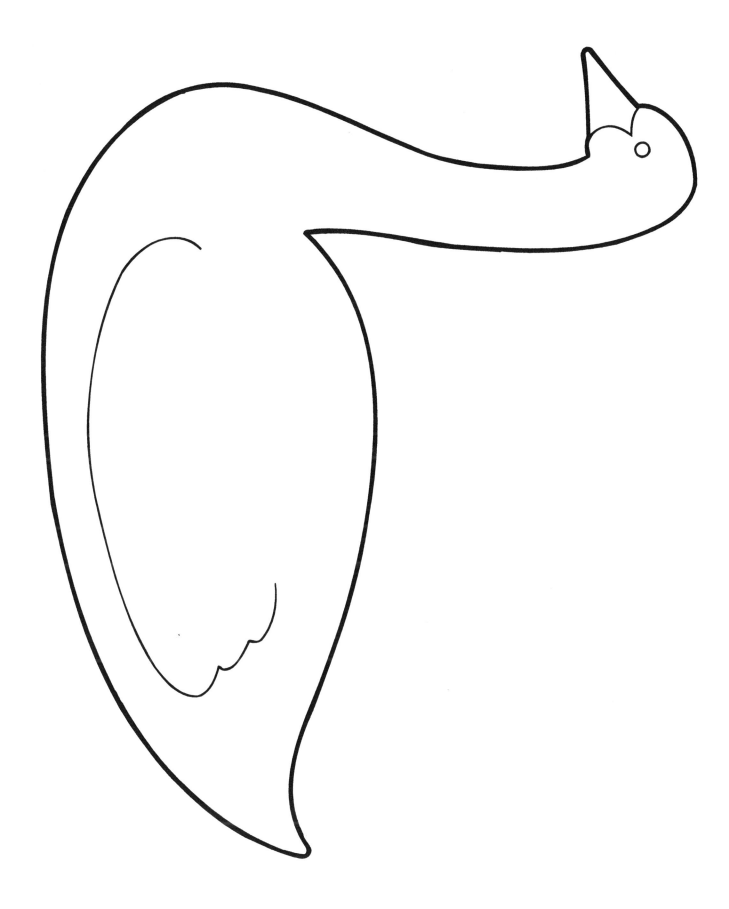

Swan 203

Swan 205

Tiger   207

Tiger 209

Triceratops 211

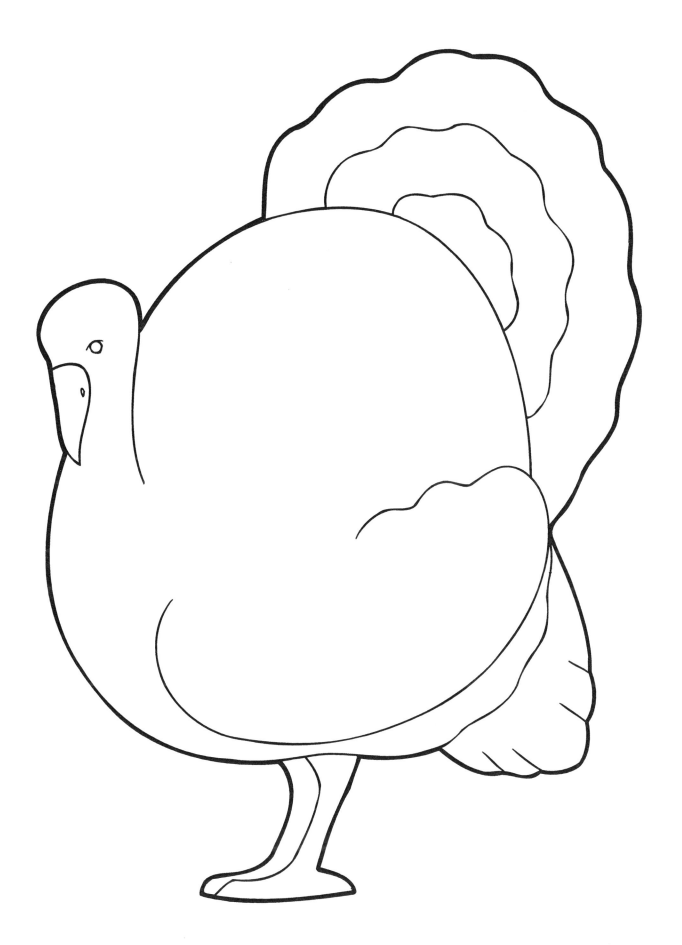

Turkey 215

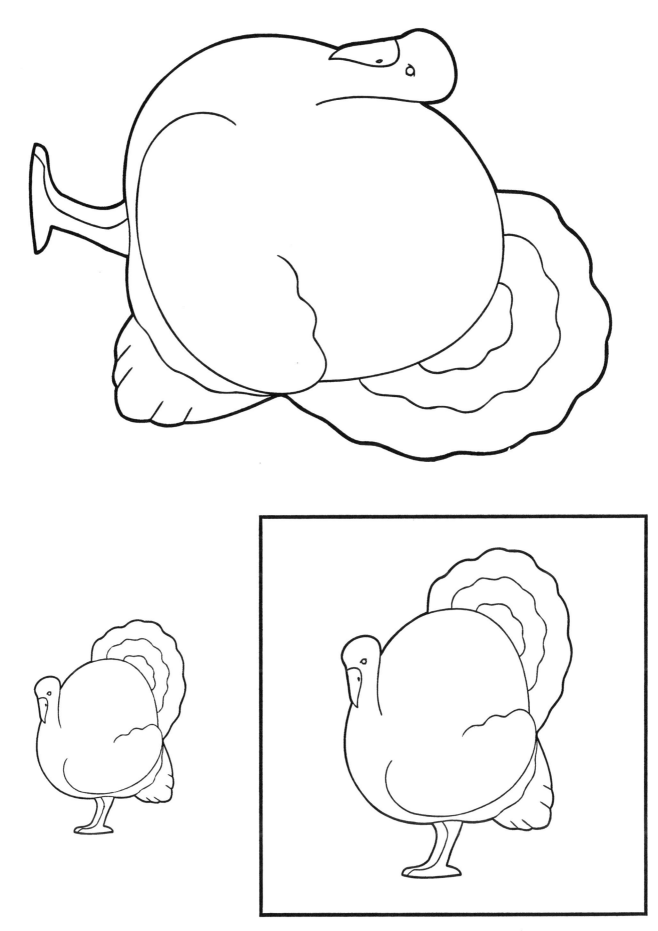

Turkey 217

Tyrannosaurus 223

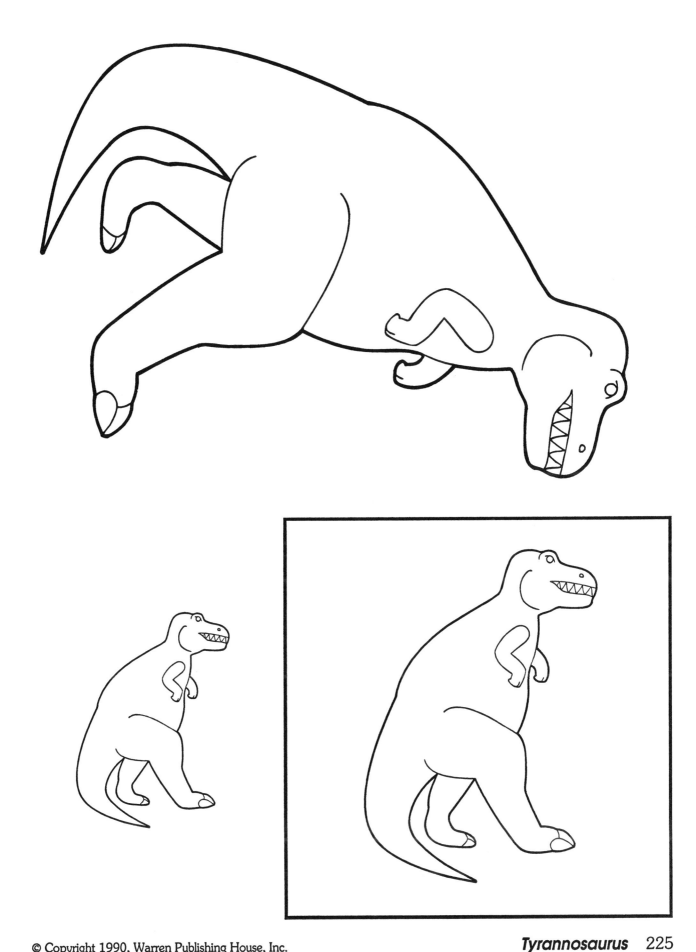

Tyrannosaurus 225

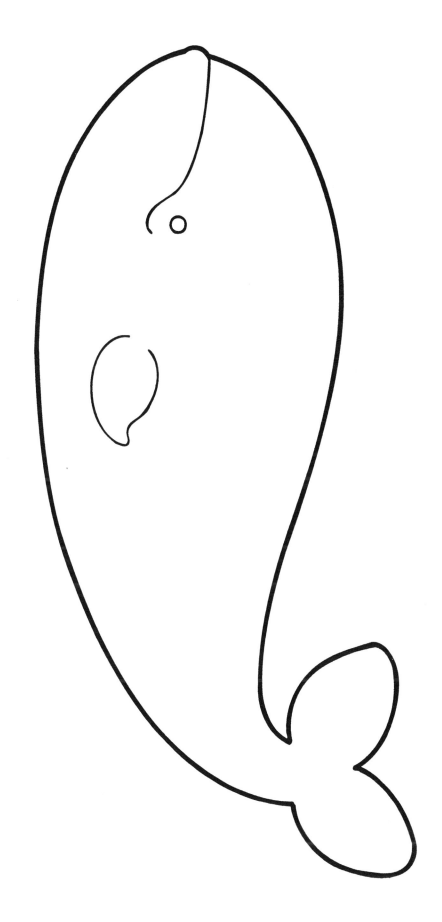

Whale 227

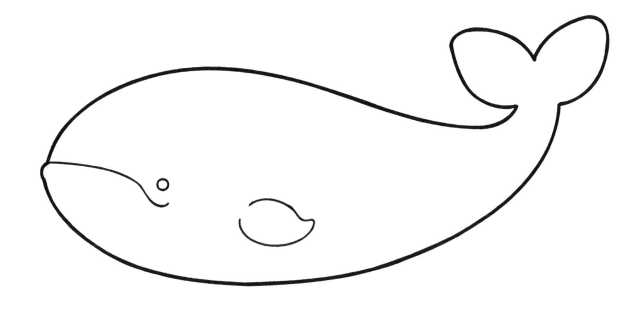

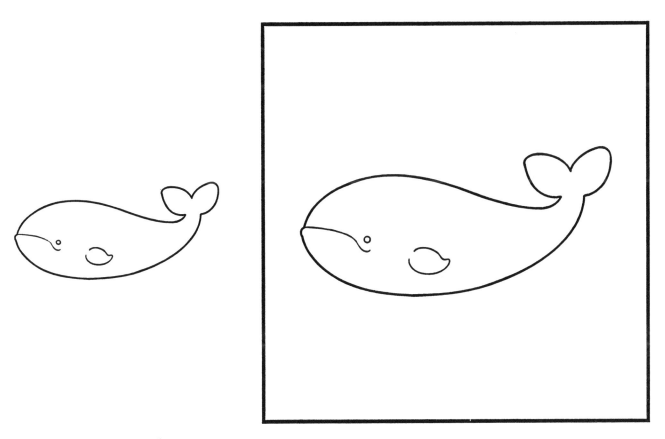

Whale 229

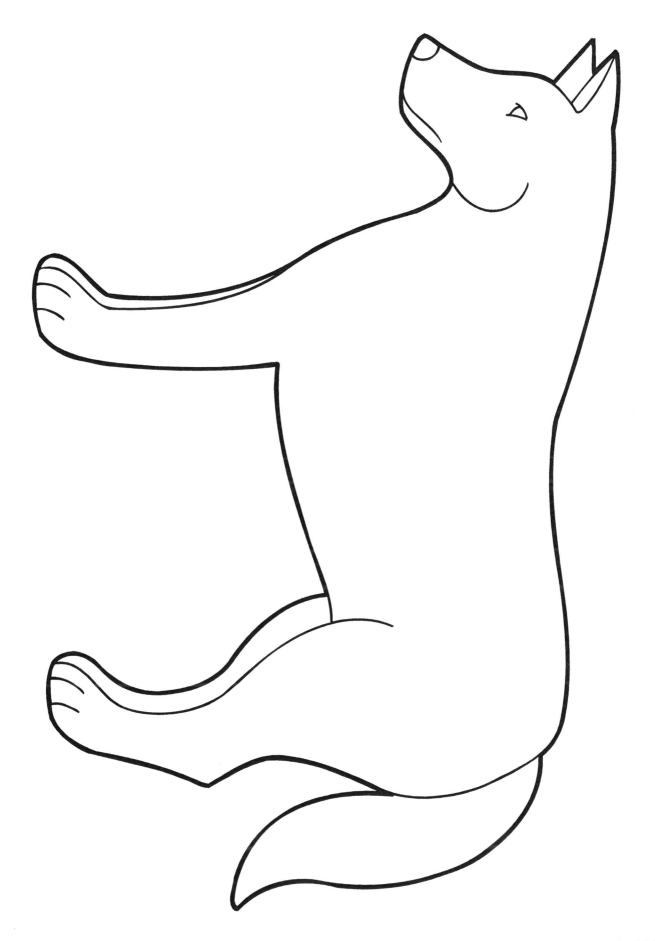

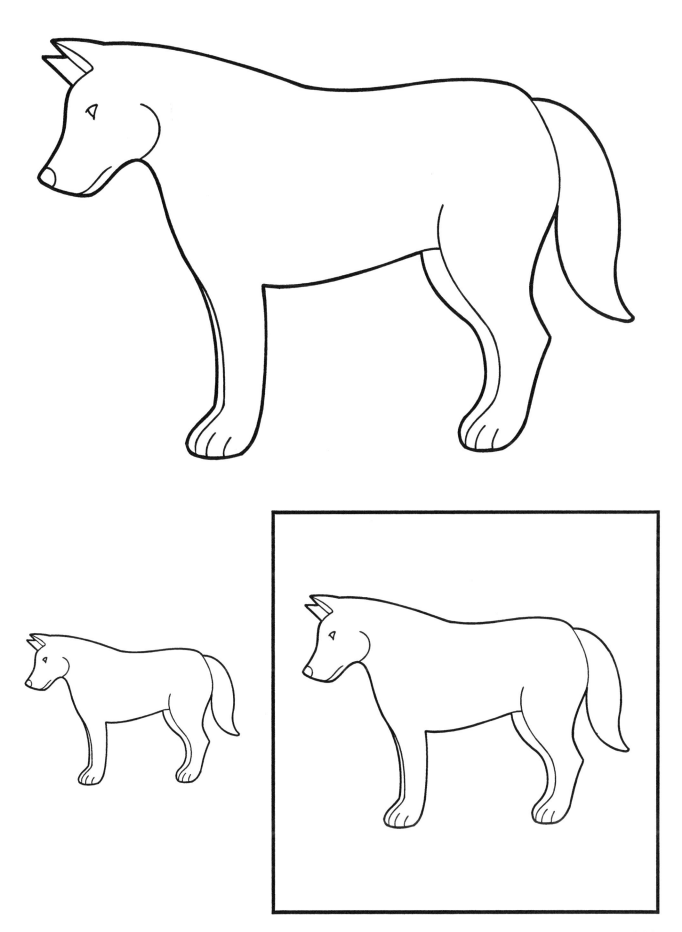

Wolf 233

Zebra 237

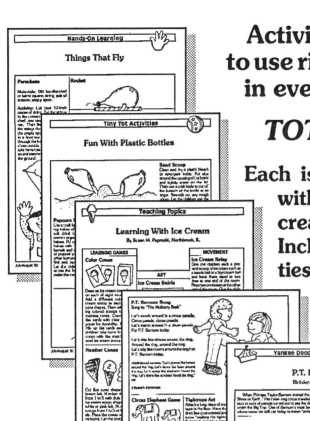

Activities, songs and new ideas to use right now are waiting for you in every issue of the

TOTLINE® NEWSLETTER.

Each issue puts the fun into teaching with 32 pages of challenging and creative activities for young children. Included are open-ended art activities, learning games, music, language and science activities plus 8 reproducible pattern pages.

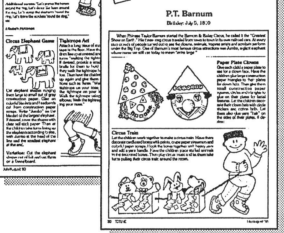

Sample Issue $2.00

You'll find the *Totline® Newsletter* an indispensable source of fresh new ideas. Page for page, there are more usable activities in this newsletter than in any other early childhood education newsletter.

"Out of all the materials on the market today, I find your resources are what I use."

"...The ideas are very refreshing."

"It's the finest magazine for the preschool teachers that I've found in my 12 years of teaching."

"For my money spent, I get more ideas from your newsletter than any other publication I receive."

"I love the Totline® Newsletter. I just keep finding new resources and ideas to keep me fresh."

Totline Books

Super Snacks - 120 seasonal sugarless snack recipes kids love.

Teaching Tips - 300 helpful hints for working with young children.

Teaching Toys - over 100 toy and game ideas for teaching learning concepts.

Piggyback Songs - 110 original songs, sung to the tunes of childhood favorites.

More Piggyback Songs - 195 more original songs.

Piggyback Songs for Infants and Toddlers - 160 original songs, for infants and toddlers.

Piggyback Songs in Praise of God - 185 original religious songs, sung to familiar tunes.

Piggyback Songs in Praise of Jesus - 240 more original religious songs.

Holiday Piggyback Songs - over 240 original holiday songs.

Animal Piggyback Songs - over 200 original songs about animals.

1·2·3 Art - over 200 open-ended art activities.

1·2·3 Games - 70 no-lose games to ages 2 to 8.

1·2·3 Colors - over 500 Color Day activities for young children.

1·2·3 Puppets - over 50 puppets to make for working with young children.

1·2·3 Murals - over 50 murals to make with children's open-ended art.

1·2·3 Books - over 20 beginning concept books to make for working with young children.

Teeny-Tiny Folktales - 15 folktales from around the world plus flannelboard patterns.

Short-Short Stories - 18 original stories plus seasonal activities.

Mini-Mini Musicals - 10 simple musicals, sung to familiar tunes.

Small World Celebrations - 16 holidays from around the world to celebrate with young children.

Special Day Celebrations - 55 mini celebrations for holidays and special events.

Yankee Doodle Birthday Celebrations - activity ideas for celebrating birthdays of 30 famous Americans.

"Cut & Tell" Scissor Stories for Fall - 8 original stories plus patterns.

"Cut & Tell" Scissor Stories for Winter - 8 original stories plus patterns.

"Cut & Tell" Scissor Stories for Spring - 8 original stories plus patterns.

Seasonal Fun - 50 two-sided reproducible parent flyers.

Theme-A-Saurus - the great big book of mini teaching themes.

Theme-A-Saurus II - the great big book of more mini teaching themes.

Alphabet and Number Rhymes - reproducible take-home books.

Color, Shape & Season Rhymes - reproducible take-home books.

Object Rhymes - reproducible take-home books about seasonal objects such as hearts, pumpkins and turkeys.

Animal Rhymes - reproducible pre-reading books using repetition and rhyme about animals.

Our World - more than 120 easy environmental activities.

"Mix & Match" Animal Patterns - multi-sized patterns for 58 different animals.

"Mix & Match" Everyday Patterns - multi-sized patterns for 58 different everyday objects.

"Mix & Match" Nature Patterns - multi-sized patterns for 58 different nature objects.

Available at school supply stores and parent/teacher stores or write for our *FREE* catalog.

Warren Publishing House, Inc. • **P.O. Box 2250, Dept. B** • **Everett, WA 98203**